Beloved Idea

Also by Ann Killough:

Sinners in the Hands: Selections from the Catalog

Beloved Idea

ANN KILLOUGH

Alice James Books

FARMINGTON, MAINE

10 9 8 7 6 5 4 3 2 1

Alice James Books are published by Alice James Poetry Cooperative, Inc., an affiliate of the University of Maine at Farmington.

ALICE JAMES BOOKS
238 MAIN STREET
FARMINGTON, ME 04938

www.alicejamesbooks.org

Library of Congress Cataloging-in-Publication Data
Killough, Ann
Beloved idea / Ann Killough.
    p.   cm.
ISBN-13: 978-1-882295-65-4
ISBN-10: 1-882295-65-X
I. Title.
PS3611.I452B45 2007
811'.6--dc22   2007025122

Alice James Books gratefully acknowledges support from the University of Maine at Farmington and the National Endowment for the Arts. ❧

Cover Art: ©Jake Rajs
www.jakerajs.com

Note: The italicized words in "[(the) horsemen]" are from Faulkner's *Light in August*.

for Joe

CONTENTS

ACKNOWLEDGMENTS

Grateful acknowledgment is made to the editors of the following journals, in which some of these poems first appeared (sometimes in different form and under different titles).

Field: "[gulag]"
The Massachusetts Review: "[Statue of Liberty]"
Salamander: "[white whale]" (under the title "[the white whale]");
   "[the boy and the slave on the raft]"; "[stuffed animal]" (under the title
   "[in sheep's clothing]")

This book is an offering to my parents, William and Mary Joslin, from whom I inherited my political despair and hope.

It also honors my remarkable undergraduate teacher Susan Gilbert, who first guided me into the bizarre and deadly territory of our nation's ideas about itself.

Others I would like to thank, of those many friends and teachers who have helped me along the way, are the irreplaceable Eva Bourke and the whole William Joiner Center community; my coworkers Susan Roberts and Aimee Sands of the Brookline Poetry Series and all the gang there; John Anderson, Jennifer Barber, Susan Nisenbaum Becker, Betty Buchsbaum, Ellen Donoghue, Kathrine Douthit, Terry Jane England, Kim Garcia, Rebecca Kaiser Gibson, David Green, Jim Henle, Jennifer Johnson, Nancy Kassel, Frannie Lindsay, Michael Mack, Liz Moore, Tam Lin Neville, Laura Nooney, Dawn Paul, Claire Robson, Natasha Saje, Catherine Sasanov, Bert Stern, Christine Tierney, Lisa Vaas, Afaa Michael Weaver, Gordon Weissmann, Gary Whited and many others, including all the fabulous Alices and the brilliant, tireless April and Lacy.

As always I am grateful for my splendid daughters and for my brothers and sisters, who never seem to give up on me. And for Joe, who is everything.

Beloved Idea

[THE WOUND]

She took up the metaphor of the wound as if it were a newborn baby with something terribly wrong with its spine.

She knew it was her own baby and yet manifestly planetary, with referents drifting above it like dust from an invisible landscape.

She knew the most important thing about the metaphor of the wound was that it never healed.

And that it seemed to function as some sort of insertion into the argument, perhaps into every argument, as the precious unknown of the major premise of perhaps every argument.

Like a kind of Christ Child of every argument.

As though every argument were a stable full of domestic animals chewing their preordained fodder intersected by a series of shepherds and kings arranging themselves in relation to an almost completely swaddled but infinite metaphor.

*

Unspeakable opening.

*

So now it seemed maybe there was actually a body of metaphors almost indistinguishable from each other.

The metaphor of the wound and the metaphor of the unspeakable opening and the metaphor of the inevitable sacrifice, for example, that she would prefer not to touch even with theological gloves on, a figurative body of terrible relatives in which each organ cooperated in keeping the enormous tumor of understanding in place that grew from the metaphorical body like an obscene appendage.

The body politic, for example.

The metaphor of the body politic itself being cruelly deceptive except that there was no way of really knowing that.

She was beginning to feel trapped.

She ran down the street of her poem yelling with metaphors flying out behind her like flames.

With metaphors crawling out of her chest and mouth like gigantic beetles, and out of her one good eye.

*

When the mob gathered and wrestled her to the ground she just kept yelling and pointing at visible articles of metaphor. The metaphor of the mob, for example, and of the ground, which was so repulsively comforting. She knew the metaphor of the wound was still safe in her poem, which was turning out to be a manger like all the others.

As though the poem had begun to cooperate with the authorities behind her back, which it undoubtedly had.

[BODY IN EVIDENCE]

She imagined the body in the exact middle of the evidence like a spider in its web.

Or perhaps like the prey still struggling incoherently over to one side of the web with the inward threads of the spider around it already seeming like its own unbearable guts.

*

Of course in her case the body turned out to be the body of the beloved idea of her nation.

Which seemed always of a different order than the fabric of ideological evidence, within which it hung like a lynched man.

Its main characteristic being intrusion, a helpless intrusive quality against which it turned out that the evidence had been organized all along and which was the only thing that remained incomprehensible.

Its main characteristic being a kind of mute surplus over all possible results to be obtained by its entrapment in the vast matrix of metaphors that she could now see stretching out on all sides infinitely.

The endlessly proliferating suburbs of entrepreneurial fabulist historical high-voltage gridlock sewage metaphoricity of the gluttonous national evangelism of understanding.

Within which the beloved idea hung like a lost sheep.

*

She was aware that her love for it was a naked thing.

Poor, universal.

She couldn't help it, it was all she had.

[STUFFED ANIMAL]

She had written her book which was essentially a metaphor in sheep's clothing.

The beloved nation's body as the idea of a wolf with all the most delicate organs of predation and her desire upon it like layers of a poorly fitting disguise.

Looking more or less like a normal book, or at least like a stuffed animal.

A transitional object.

She was planning to walk out into the world with the book under her arm like Dorothy with Toto or the Cowardly Lion caressing the tip of his delightful tail.

She was convinced she was not the Witch.

*

She herself did not want to pose as a sheep.

She herself did not want to be the Good Shepherd and end up hanging on the cross like the trophy of a tournament gone seriously awry.

A tournament indistinguishable from the way the beloved nation had come upon her idea of it fully armed like an unscrupulous redeemer.

The way it had acted.

A tournament indistinguishable from the fight over the body of reality which she had originally set out to represent.

Whatever that was.

*

She realized she liked the notion of the beloved nation's armor and its cozy relationship to the notion of sheep's clothing a little too much.

She was too attached to the idea of the body beneath.

To memory in general, which was always pressing its case in the most obsequious way, offering precious tidbits of the beloved nation's amazing grace as if they had some kind of continual being.

Taking upon itself the identity of the devoted servant as if the idea of identity were not already a wizard dressed up in rags and wandering around Oz like a demented scarecrow.

Hoping for a handout from the Lord, or at least from Auntie Em, who was a metaphor for something nobody wanted to look at too closely for fear it might turn out to be home.

*

Each poem was essentially a cry for help.

And had a way of pretending not to be what it had already pretended to be, which was a disguise in the form of a wolf.

She kept coming back to the idea of a wolf. Maybe she liked it because wolves seemed so historically misunderstood and essential. As well as the fact that they traveled in packs with ferocious hierarchy.

She imagined the beloved nation with its sheep's face and the other wolves around it like dependent clauses. Or the other dependent clauses around it like sheep.

She could never keep straight who was who in the sentences. At times she felt like a simple noun in apposition, Red Riding Hood's grandmother hiding in the closet or the first witch with only her red shoes sticking out.

*

She knew that each poem was essentially the same as all the others.

And that each was an attempt not so much to avoid despair as to figure out which church it was ultimately the organ of.

She knew the nation was already written over like a newspaper with universal love stories and pleas for criminal justice.

But somehow this was not enough for her, she wanted reality to emerge from the embrace of her poems like a freshly laid metaphor.

She wanted everything.

[WHITE WHALE]

It was not just the whiteness of the whale's skin but what was written on it.

The hereditary scars.

The way they appeared of their own accord more and more forming a network of incomprehensible commandments.

*

She knew that the metaphor of the whale continued to patrol the coastal waters of her national imagination like a restless lover.

And that the hunt for it seemed to be repetitive, and compulsive.

And that each hunt ended up bound to the whale by the difficult rope of its own discursive harpoon and that grievous human suffering was usually involved.

*

She knew that one likely referent for the whale was the leviathan obsessions of the entire metaphorical body of her nation.

With its vast apparatus of conquest and its high-frequency cries of longing.

Into which the figures of individual speech were continually being swallowed like an encyclopedic series of phosphorescent microscopic organisms or Biblical prophets.

*

But that at the same time the whale was also in reference to some alternate and dreadfully impinging state of things.

That it was not just exhaustive and inexhaustible but possessed of some mute and terrible reality that was the object of infinite national desire.

So that the figure of Ishmael alone in the water became more and more important to her.

*

As though Ishmael were a kind of reduction of the whale to some secular remnant.

As though by clinging to Ishmael she might have some kind of reduced hope for the release of her nation, or at least for the salvage of a traumatized but serviceable discourse of relative sanity.

As though relative sanity were what her nation actually wanted, or ever had.

[U N D E R P A N T S]

Underpants as necessarily referring to the manly underpants of startling size that regularly were hanging in a row on the porch across the alley from her bedroom.

As though a row of overweight fathers had flown through Brookline in their underpants and gotten caught in a clothesline.

The kind of fathers that run the world by means of secret meetings on every continent flying over the seven seas in formation like Canada geese.

But that now had to fly with no underpants, their international penises hanging down like unusable landing gear.

*

She always rejoiced at the sight of the underpants.

They seemed to offer a kind of hope, although she wasn't sure what.

Perhaps the kind of hope that is normally offered by undergarments hanging on a clothesline with their seamed faces broadcasting a story of organized and intimate renewal.

Of how somebody is thinking ahead.

*

Or perhaps the hope was more foundational, so to speak, and had to do with the sturdiness of the operation that produced the recurrent row of underpants.

Not just the dependably loud and Russian argumentation out of which the underpants appeared to be extruded like a row of continuing and faithful facts, but also the unvarying style and whiteness of the underpants.

As if they were a testament to some rigorous belief, perhaps in the absolute.

Perhaps just in the indisputable rightness of at least one thing.

*

Which brought her back to the migrating fathers in the original hypothesis and what it was exactly they had lost.

What it was exactly they had left innocently hanging across from her like a succession of mute and outmoded pronouns.

Like a succession of hopes of protection from the humiliation of nakedness, a succession of humiliatingly naked and public hopes.

Without which they flew shamelessly over the seven seas but would never again be able to land.

She carried the metaphor of the astronaut around with her like a
radioactive pocketbook.

A pocketbook whose principal referent was herself, of course, or else
possibly some kind of clothing, a pocketbook that could unfold itself into
a silver raiment, for example, with a lining that was a relief map of her
entire nation and fitted her body like the leotard of an overweight dancer.

As though she might be skinless without it, or at least without the idea of
the entire nation sliding against her internal organs and the effulgence of
her exile on its other side like a new moon.

Exile being a constant travail but also a sort of floating away from the
spaceship with only an umbilical cord made up entirely of the unknown
necessities of history.

She was frightened, much of the time.

She missed her sister, who was at all times far away with her own layers of
metaphor buttoned up tight to her throat and her hands tied behind her
back with theological string.

And her brother, who was wearing a costume made entirely of *The New
York Times.*

She turned her face outward toward the stars. There were other
astronauts floating on either side of her but none of them looked at her.

She remembered the metaphor of home, but could not remember its
referents, or exactly how it was configured. Whether it was just a
pocketbook lined with astronauts spread out into an inaudible scream
like the skin of angels.

[OCTOPUS]

There was another love poem
about her nation as an octopus
but she wasn't sure how it would work out.

She didn't want it to partake only of the obvious,
with the arms standing for everything,
and yet the scope of the arms was undeniable,
their way of indicating a necessary plurality of means,
not to mention ends.

The swimming seemed part of it, the way her nation
might swim dreamily and in slow motion
through the seas of desire in a multiply phallic way
(the arms again) as if it were entirely unmoored
from any of the normal gravitational means
of support and debility and were already completely lost
in the world of its own insignificant prey.

It distressed her the way she was unable to repeat its name
because it was the wrong name,
like the time at the Aquarium when a child pointed out scornfully
that what she thought was a baby octopus didn't have a head
and so was probably a starfish, starfish not being the right metaphor
for anything, and especially not her nation, her feeling for her nation,
which clearly did not have a head or even enough arms
to be a real metaphorical octopus,
so that the poem seemed essentially impossible,
not just for that reason, but because there was something wrong
with its very organs, with the internal impulse
that was driving it through the desperate waters of the page,
some kind of shoddy escapism maybe, a Disney quality.

She didn't know what to do about metaphors, she really didn't.

They were so demanding,
and delivered so little in the end,
and yet one was still obsessed by them, seeing an octopus
every time one closed one's eyes or said the wrong name,
feeling its soft suckered arms against one's skin,
especially the skin of one's face, one's mouth,
inside one's mouth and down one's throat
over and over, like the reversal of creation.

[SNAKE IN THE CAN]

It was not clear which part of her dilemma was the snake and which was the can.

It was not clear if she herself was the snake or perhaps some part of the snake, the skin of the snake for example already slipping away from the snake per se like a disproved theory.

*

There was always the possibility that the snake was purely phallic in nature. That the snake was a kind of duly elected representative of some kind of surgically removed idea of potency and differentiation carefully repackaged for delicious consumption.

In that case she definitely did not want her dilemma to be solely the can.

She wanted whatever meat remained in the incessantly emergent formulation to have something to do with an irreducible object of inquiry on her part.

*

As though the meat were preexistent.

As though her longing were like a little woman inserted into the can that was clinging to the snake in a fierce but tiny bear hug and waiting for the moment when the can would open and the snake would spring out like a rocket ship that was really only a practical joke.

As though her longing did not care about the practical joke as long as it could keep clinging and clinging to the prepackaged idea of a longing worth clinging to.

She was interested in the river, in how the river presented itself as an inexhaustible body of signification.

Or rather as some kind of originary and ultimately unsignifiable body on which the bodies of boy and slave and raft floated like the flimsy historical compound metaphor she knew they were.

As though the only proper approach to the metaphor of the river were a sort of veneration.

While any number of approaches to the boy and slave and raft might meet with approval in the highest circles.

*

And yet she knew that the most important element in the mechanics of the operation in its entirety was the river.

That without the river and its wandering and intractable excess the historical parasitism of the boy and slave and raft would be unable to refer even to itself, let alone to all the Americanized versions of unassimilable longings it was traditionally made to refer to.

She herself was always the raft.

She enjoyed the feeling of the infinite surface of the river against the underside of her body and the tender weight of the boy and the slave on the surface of her understanding like folded wings.

*

The story itself seemed ultimately inessential. As opposed to its protagonist, the starry and intricate metaphor that had long since escaped the story and taken its place in the army of national and international misapprehension that was always engaging in a new and horrifying campaign.

Her only hope was the river.

She went back to the river and lay herself down like an incomplete metaphor and closed her eyes.

She could hear across the water the clash of referents. It sounded as if a couple of them might be heading her way.

[DETERRENCE]

The referents rush joyously toward the scene of the catastrophe.

As though it were the scene of maximum security discursive fusion.

As though it were the Veil.

*

They think catastrophe is as if discourse had gone into a coma.

As if it had shown up at the site and everyone had strapped it down for the operation.

As if they had wired each of its internal organs for sanctification.

*

(BAM!)

*

(Discourse itself meanwhile having a dream

[INFORMATION]

She kept getting the feeling that information might be a form of catastrophe, like television.

Parallel geometries of need.

The face of the accuser and the face of the accused evacuated together, twin towers.

*

She did know there was an architecture of contagion.

And that if you knew the right angle you could glide into the intersecting and suspended layers of metaphor like a sacrificial aircraft.

The high altar, incessant supplication.

*

A catastrophe always being a kind of answer.

Not just to the politics of homicide but also of course to the agony of deferral.

The panic of deterrence.

*

The holocaust of means being essential, the hemorrhage of ordinary means.

The hemorrhage of reality.

Information.

*

She was most impressed by the dissemination of everything.

How all exits were blocked by the fiery fuselage of evidence.

How no matter what happened somebody always ended up screaming all the way down.

The holy ghost being the remainder of the body of the departed god.

She thought again of television, which seemed like the site of a terrible annihilation and at the same time was always whispering from across the room like an underground river.

The holy ghost being multiple, and of a great congregation.

*

The holy ghost being the remainder of the evacuated body politic, the holy ghost as the aggregate body of the consumed, for example, and of their consumers. The television audience.

The holy ghost as the remainder in the form of a garment. The costume of the holy ghost, the holy ghost as the reminder of the great congregation of the virtually naked.

What it means to love the holy ghost.

*

She remembered the story of how they gathered in the Bible and the holy ghost came upon them as tongues of fire. The holy ghost as the actual process of consumption.

The question always being about the departed body. What is it?

Sometimes she thought in terms of a love story. How the story itself becomes the garment, and the process of its own consumption. The site of an annihilation, beloved, beloved.

*

Because she wanted to understand her nation. What the body was it continued to love in the form of a mob of ghostly and numberless desires.

Of a cloud of desires gathered around the site of the continual loss of something.

What is it?

[(THE) HORSEMEN]

they come galloping out of the Good Book like metaphors gone
completely amok

the faces of the horses are immaterial, the motive of the riders is
immaterial

what happens is the people's desire for them

*

oh her nation just loves it imaginary

the end metastasis of the imaginary of the

end

end

*

end

*

*through which from the study window he watches the so hidden
sign which he calls his* operational destitution *monument* the nation rushes
toward the site where were last seen [(the) horsemen]

and falls into a deep sleep

there's no place like home

*

in the formal and topological sense however she still has hope

and thus like the godfather at the end of her poem beheads the horses

one by one and leaves them in the bed of her nation wake up screaming

my darlings wake up little Susie

[Statue of Liberty]

And yet we suspect that our relationship to the Statue of Liberty is not simple.

That we are expecting something from her which she is secretly no longer providing.

That she is actually undermining our entire sense of ourselves, not only collectively but individually.

What do you think?

I mean really.

No fair coming up with that stuff about the symbol of our nation or our nation's delusions about its own saintly welcoming qualities or anything to do with France.

Think in terms of if aliens had already contacted the Statue of Liberty and she were receiving transmissions across the whole surface of her copper body which she were greatly enjoying after all those years of nothing but runny condensations.

Think in terms of what the aliens might have in mind.

Would they care that she was hollow and full of stairs?

Would they care that she was too big to be happy?

*

So now what if the Statue of Liberty has found out that she can move and is only waiting for the right moment?

What if there are beginning to be words in her book, more and more words on the coppery pages, the ones that do not turn, or not yet?

What if she is beginning to feel the horror of her position, the way she has no peers or even anyone who understands that she is in the tradition of the enormous destroyer?

What is it she is becoming convinced she must destroy?

*

So now picture what you think the Statue of Liberty might destroy and realize that you are not right.

That whatever you thought of is not it, or at least not quite it and certainly not all of it.

That you have no idea what she is thinking, or at least not a complete idea.

That the very nature of her body renders her susceptible not only to alien transmissions but to all the transmissions of the earth.

That she is a kind of Pole along with the North and South ones and draws the magnetic fields of the earth toward herself like shiploads of huddled immigrants and reads them like ticker tape inside her spiky head.

That she feels what you feel but much more of it.

That she sees what you see but the backside of it as well, the side you will never see.

That she has already begun to change something even in you, even in me.

That we already know what it is.

[BREAKING AND ENTERING]

In order for this very important metaphor to work there must first be a sanctuary.

In the sanctuary there must be an imaginary of radiance, incarnation of some irreversible kind.

Livestock, the chewing of luminous fodder. The mall, for example.

*

The metaphor of the intruder comes in by the back door.

It is like a response to the question incessantly circulating in the claustral space of the sanctuary.

Or maybe it is the question itself in its natural body, like a naked repair man.

*

There is breakage.

As of glass, there is necessary and finite breakage, a kind of instrumental sacrifice of a material that may or may not be asking for it.

Fundamental weaponry.

*

The problem with the metaphor of breaking and entering comes when it begins to cannibalize itself.

When the intruders begin to pile up inside the sanctuary like very livestock eating each other and exclaiming over the luminosity of their own flesh.

Metastasis of the delicious wound.

*

Meanwhile she was hoping people wouldn't ask her about referents for the metaphor of breaking and entering.

She was hoping they would think of examples from their own life and wouldn't expect her poem to become the kind of sanctuary that leaves the back door unlocked.

That sits on its own sofa in its best negligee with a self-satisfied grin on its face.

*

Neither did she want her poem to play into the hands of the terrorists.

To become one of those sanctuaries out of whose reverend arches intruders lob discursive monstrosities into the peaceful streets.

So that a religious leader has to step in and save things.

*

Of course there was a good chance that it was too late.

That the sanctuary of her poem's intent had already been breached by some goofy and ravenous band of angels.

Sweet chariot, and that they had already carried it home.

[PROSTHESIS]

She was interested in the metaphor of prosthesis because it implied an original and nostalgic body for which the prosthesis was a substitution or extension.

A way to signal that something was missing.

Amputation.

*

For example, a national tragedy as a kind of disappearance and then the search for a prosthesis. That which could police the site, supplement, satellitic.

Or a national tragedy as the prosthesis itself, substitution.

The prosthesis as a double. As a robot attached to the original and nostalgic body dragging it along screaming toward the site.

*

Eternal twinning.

War as a prosthesis. The prosthesis as clone, war as a clone of the nostalgic body of war.

The prosthesis as a cancerous metastasis of the nostalgic base formula.

*

So why did she bring this up again? Love as a prosthesis?

The idea of the beloved as the prosthetic robot dragging the body of nostalgia toward the site of the original amputation, screaming?

Eternal twinning, cancerous metastases etcetera?

*

The remainder. Prosthesis as the remainder.

That which is extruded by the natural operation of tragedy.

The idea of love as the remainder.

[GRAMMAR]

So then she began opening the drawers of grammar desperately looking for more and more metaphors.

The silver chest of English grammar with its stacks of ancestral utensils and its lining like the inside of a beloved animal she began to open like a Yankee officer come upon the hidden cache.

The one the Confederate family had buried under the pigsty and the pig had dreamed above like a hen on its imaginary nest.

The stacks of nouns, the verbs like a row of delicate dinner forks, the monogrammed adjectives.

The conditional clauses like serving spoons, the magnificent carving knife which she began to fondle like the exhausted Yankee officer longing for home although she wasn't sure what it might be a metaphor for.

The pig long slaughtered and gone to feed the remnants of the regiment from Ohio.

The regiment from Ohio beginning to seem like a stand-in for the many Midwestern fundamentalists who had moved into her hometown in North Carolina and eaten up the remains of the liberals like spareribs.

So that the grammar began to seem to want to be a series of theories about history, and about Raleigh.

Which she was loathe to let it be.

2

So that she went back to the body of grammar, the vehicle of grammar as a possible means of proceeding.

The ramshackle vehicle of grammar with her poem as the driver, the metaphor of her pocketbook lying in the poem's lap like a beating heart.

Her poem rushing the pocketbook to the hospital in order to save something, maybe her own cosmetic paraphernalia, or maybe not.

Maybe the vehicle of grammar as more like an old Chevy rusting at the dump with the remains of a baby bottle on the floor of the back seat.

The bottle of a baby who had long since grown up and become notorious and whom everybody in his hometown had always thought was most likely to succeed.

So that he now became a metaphor for the beloved nation whose body was probably the one her poem was rushing to the hospital.

As if she could save it, as if all it had ever needed was what her poem was about to arrive holding forth with a big flashy grin like one of the Magi.

As if its body had always been a baby hollowed out into the most inhuman metaphor conceivable and laid down in the straw.

3

The straw now seeming the way to proceed.

The beloved nation's body now seeming to be represented not only by the baby but by the straw under it that having been hollowed out by the pressure of potential redemption was no longer edible by a beast of burden.

By the rows of assorted animals who were now delegated the role of merely looking on, and did.

So that she wanted to draw a parallel with the metaphor of silverware, the rows of assorted spoons and forks lined up in the darkness under the pigsty with the pig already being dragged toward its meaningless and eternal sacrifice.

The Yankee officer already opening the box, the assorted possibilities already beginning to announce themselves to him in a cacophony of useful metaphors that had nothing to do with the terrible squealing.

The beloved nation's body being perhaps the box itself, or perhaps not.

The usefulness of the beloved nation's body beginning to seem now like the problem, the transcendent submissiveness of it in the Yankee officer's arms.

The way the Yankee officer was now walking slowly back toward the ruined house, with his horse watching him from under a tree.

The beloved nation's body as that horse.

4

So that of course what the Yankee officer would meet in the ruined house would be the starved Southern lady.

The one with the secreted pistol from the Revolutionary War in which the Southern lady's favorite grandfather had been a common soldier.

The meeting on the stairs.

The Yankee officer holding the chest of silver against his breast like a bulletproof vest.

The whole scene clearly a tableau of her love for her nation, with all the parts completely interchangeable.

The nation most obviously as the pistol, or most obviously as the stairs themselves.

Her intention most obviously as the lady's gaze, or as the exhausted officer's perception of the lady's gaze, or most obviously as the exhausted officer's overdetermined attachment to the silverware.

So that the moral of the story begins to come out all over the place, like the fires that the remnants of the regiment from Ohio are now starting.

The radically untrustworthy moral with its incendiary corollaries, the useless and despicable moral sneaking in the back door of the fire metaphor like a raccoon, looking for food.

5

The regiment from Ohio spreading out now into the surrounding countryside, the regiment from Ohio being unsuitable as a metaphor for anything that bodes well.

The surrounding countryside looking a lot like the flat fields around her mother's South Carolina hometown, the regiment from Ohio therefore beginning to have some figurative relationship to memory.

Memory thus suddenly rearing its ugly and omnivorous head which is yet helplessly desired, like the terrible head of the beloved nation.

Its teeth.

Like the box of silverware, like the stacks of invaluable substitutions in the original mouth of the box carried across the yard by the officer in a blue uniform indistinguishable from the infinite substitutions of history. Like the pig, so eatable.

The rows of ribs and the still beating heart, the eyes still gazing into hers even as they fade into the infinite substitutions of ideology.

The remnants of the regiment from Ohio now triumphant.

The flat field of her memory now set afire by the remnants of the regiment from Ohio, the fire spreading toward a ramshackle trailer on the edge of that field with petunias planted in coffee cans on the front steps. Her love for her nation taking its final resting place among those coffee cans.

[GARDEN]

The metaphor of the garden was beginning to be one of her concerns.

The way it was so glamorous, so continually set up as the originary metaphor with hundreds of referents drawn into its vicinity like pilgrims camping out in the suburbs of Jerusalem.

Like pilgrims telling stories around their caravans of someone dressed in a rose bush who purposely caught fire.

Who could not stop dancing.

*

She thought perhaps it was the wall.

That perhaps the metaphorical wall around the garden was the element that aroused people to stylized violence.

That made them want to deposit their ideological ordnance inside the garden and make a clean getaway.

She imagined the referents arriving at the gate like Sherman tanks.

*

Or maybe it was the gate.

The gate as the orifice of the metaphor where the attending angel stood dressed in the clothing of ordinary desire.

Holding a trowel or some other gardening tool in the shape of a flaming sword.

The glimpse of the garden behind him, the fabulous Tree.

*

Of course it was the Tree.

Although she suspected that the Tree itself had long since shed its unbearable fruit and branched out into new territory.

That it had sent typological roots far out under the wall and essentially emptied itself of all proximate usefulness in the interest of some entirely other figurative idea.

So that the whole garden was like an abandoned commercial establishment that the customers continued to visit out of a kind of historically accurate depravity.

*

Her idea was that the garden should be left alone.

That if one feels compelled to pursue a glorious metaphor and defoliate the hell out of it one should probably go away and reexamine one's linguistic priorities.

That if one can't identify with the horticultural fatigue of a glorious metaphor one should probably go to hell.

Although the metaphor of hell was beginning to be another of her concerns.

[VEIL]

Beauty VEIL Monstrosity.

*

The Beauty of the metaphor of the Veil.

The transparency of the Beauty of the metaphor of the Veil.

The transparency of the Beauty of the metaphor of the Veil as an organ of the secreted monstrosity that the Veil is intended inevitably to make manifest.

Sacrifice, rending.

*

(The monstrous has to appear.)

(There has to be appearance at some point, right?)

*

She was interested in the metaphor of the Veil because it seemed so out of style, perhaps because of its awkward sacred quality. As if it no longer knew what it was doing attached to the head of the Bride as she boogeyed down the aisles of the late-capitalist consumerist etcetera or suddenly fell into one particular stupor.

The Veil of the Temple, the Feast of the Protective Veil of the Mother of God, why not come up and see Me some time?

*

Revelation.

*

The question that most bothered her was whether her own discursive desperation was beginning to insinuate itself into the internal chambers of the desperation of the Bride so that despite the late-capitalist consumerist etcetera and its infinite and trivial acquittals she might still end up standing in the place of the gorgeous monstrosity that is always being destroyed.

Whereupon only the discursive Veil would be left as usual but under an assumed name that might turn out to be identical to hers.

Sometimes she felt this had already happened.

*

Or that nothing could happen.

That the monstrous behind its sublime and co-created Veil was itself a kind of continual and ideological special effect.

So that capture could proceed unimpeded, for example the capture of her own national people, for example her own national people's monstrosity as a beloved Veil behind which there was nothing but perhaps their own installation as the multiple and already discursively gang-raped metaphorical Bridettes.

She couldn't do it alone. Whatever kind of rescue was called for, she couldn't do it alone.

*

(HELP!)

*

She was aware that her call for help was itself a kind of Veil.

But that she could leave that up to the discursively gallant to figure out, she knew they were on the way.

[THE ROAD]

Of course the great thing about the metaphor of the Road was that it stitched together everything.

As if everything in the mind of her nation were in some relation to a highway which was like a shoreline between two worlds.

As if there were a kind of tide of the sublime, as if there were a kind of endless asphalt pier out into the sea of those metaphors by means of which her nation understood itself as sublime.

*

The exact contents of the metaphor of the Road being less important.

Whether there were covered wagons for example or a motorcycle or some kind of imaginary van which had been painted into brutal mythological visibility and whose contents poured out of it at a moment's notice into the unsuspecting bodies of the hypothetical youth of America.

Or whether there were maybe just her, trudging along.

*

It was as if while she were trudging along the surface of the endlessly repaired and scenic metaphor she could see the tide rising under her, or maybe on one side.

The tide not only of the metaphors of sublimity but of their products, as if the products of the infernal industrial processes of the sublime were swimming in it like billions of jellyfish.

As if the whole sea were full of tentacles and beautiful transparent bodies in which miniature guts floated like primordially preserved memories, as if there were something murderously nostalgic about the whole tidal wave that was now forming right over her head.

*

Only one thing could save her but she didn't know what it was except that it had something to do with the Hero.

And not even the Hero per se but his equipment, the way he was always provided with a full set of equipment each piece of which was an irreducible object of metaphysical desire.

So that there was a wonderful sense of completion, even the sense of incompletion being present and accounted for among his accoutrements by the absent one that was always hanging there like an invisible holster full of the idea of salvation.

*

It was her nation, and she loved it.

> Pregnant women were to be referred to as "Books," and women with children as "Receipts." Men, on the other hand, were "Accounts." Exiles were "Rubbish," and prisoners undergoing investigation were "Envelopes."
>
> —*Gulag: A History,* ANNE APPLEBAUM

She felt at times as if she herself were a kind of gulag. Or the "Envelope" of a strategically metaphorical gulag such that the contents of her body were the site of a generalized panic in the form of virulent pockets of investigation.

"Rubbish" was the metaphor she was most steering clear of.

She had found that if her poem were allowed its own head it would begin to lead her to the thicket where the metaphor of "Rubbish" was waiting like a riderless horse.

*

She was drawn to Russians.

She found herself following them down the streets of Brookline, listening to their consonants as if each were a breadcrumb dropped in the terrible woods of history.

She felt like a renegade "Book," or a bird of prey.

*

It was a while before she realized that the breadcrumbs were leading her right back to "Rubbish" disguised now as a confectionery home.

Which brought up the question of the witch inside it, and who was to be held responsible.

She sat down on the doorstep while the Russians she had been following went right in.

*

She understood that she was for the most part Goldilocks.

And thus of a different discursive species than the suffering metaphors of Russian history now lying in their beds like nesting bears laid out for the inspection of the secret police.

She fingered her candy cheeks.

*

Yet it was true that the "Accounts" and "Receipts" had come home to the city of her own exile to roost.

And that each was a "Rubbish" container with the intricate furnishings of terror arranged around its walls like the bones of the kinds of domestic animals to which it was likely that she was related.

She went to the Russian store on Beacon Street and bought a witch mask.

*

She began following Russians wearing the mask.

They were not interested, they were Americans now.

She took a bite of the mask, it was delicious.

[VEHICLE]

So that by this time the metaphors had begun to seem as though in grave danger.

As though the journey they had undertaken in order to elucidate her feeling for her nation had become an epic nightmare.

In which the ground was always giving way, in which there were entire villages buried in the ground so that the wheels of the vehicle were always getting caught in something, somebody's antenna or the cross of the First Baptist Church.

Or some other construction, the straight plume of smoke arising from a house that a protagonist in some great American fiction had burned down.

The crowd of protagonists, their authenticities slung about them like weaponry, the surging crowd of protagonists following the other metaphors across the countryside like an army of deserters.

The one deserter in the crowd resembling the enemy. The relative concreteness of his person, the reassuring bulk of his vernacular equipment, the impenetrability of his intentions, so that the entire entourage began to follow him with hope and ammunition as though he might know where they would end up.

The whole operation by now like a river, perhaps like the River Styx or Jordan that someone would have to cross in order to be reunited with a beloved nation or a relatively unmediated idea of a beloved nation in order to bring it out of the Hades of discursive reality with song.

Although with no assurance of that ever being possible.

The whole operation by now an exact metaphor for the river of her comprehension, but in a suspiciously tributary way.

The ground continuing to give way and the landscape continuing to contain everything easily, as though its referent were the Lord.

As though the landscape as the Lord were the vehicle and the referent were the horizon of her love, toward which the metaphors were always advancing and which they would never attain.

The simple line of that horizon.

[REFUGE]

The arms of the metaphorical harbor which are incompletely closed.

Incomplete enclosure. The "mouth" of the refuge.

*

Two days before her birthday she was thinking of the metaphor of refuge as if it were the end of someone's story.

As if it were the metaphor at the end of the "journey" with an unyielding function like that of the uniformed guard who reminds you not to touch the glass under which lies the exhibit of glorious ephemera.

She was unhappy with the geography of the metaphor of refuge, as if the human imagination were obsessively repetitive, which she believed need not necessarily be the case.

As if the human imagination were always about to return to the idea of being very tired.

*

History of the metaphorical nest.

Hungry mouths.

*

On the day before her birthday she was thinking of the metaphor of refuge as if it were a trap. As if the animals of all the other ideas were doomed to struggle in the trap of the idea of refuge unless they could manage to gnaw off at least one of their major or minor limbs.

The animal of transcendence, for example.

As if there were no other way to provide for the hungry mouths.

Including those of the animals themselves.

*

The "mouth" of the rabbit hole.

The rabbit as prey.

*

On her birthday the focus of her worries became the permeability
of the metaphor of refuge. The way other metaphors were constantly
creeping out of its eternal folds like snakes sliding down into the waters
of the harbor.

The metaphor of escape for example. Or the metaphor of Fate. Fate as
a predator for example, as an eagle for example, an American Eagle or
perhaps just a local eagle, a kind of metaphorical Guardian Angel in the
shape of a local eagle on someone's right shoulder, perhaps that of the
President of the United States.

So that she felt that the metaphor of refuge might be in serious trouble.
But she didn't know how to rescue it, at least not by means of the
metaphor of rescue, which was now up to its own deeply dubious
activities, seeming to be one of the metaphors sliding down into the
eternal waters of the metaphor of refuge and making it less and less clean.

So that the wildlife of the metaphor were no longer protected, the
mysterious fish of beloved record for example, who had each swallowed a
gold ring of universal significance now turning belly up one by one in the
blistering universal sun.

*

The "ecological blindness" of refuge.

The abandoned lifeguard chair.

*

On the day after her birthday she was struck by the grandiosity of the metaphor of refuge, and in a very unsettling way, as if she herself had become subsumed by it. As if she herself were inside the Statue of Liberty looking out with gigantic impermeable eyes at the infernally becalmed metaphor of the harbor.

As if she herself were forced to wear the merciless copper costume and hold high the interminably delirious torch.

That was the day she began to understand the desperation of the metaphor of refuge.

How within the parameters of its own sense of national and international and especially cosmic and ideological duty it had reached the point of longing to put down its multiple incessant oars and be led solely by the current.

*

The "mouth" of the river.

The "open" sea.

Recent Titles from Alice James Books

ALICE JAMES BOOKS has been publishing exclusively poetry since 1973. One of the few presses in the country that is run collectively, the cooperative selects manuscripts for publication through both regional and national annual competitions. New regional authors become active members of the cooperative, participating in the editorial decisions of the press. The press, which historically has placed an emphasis on publishing women poets, was named for Alice James, sister of William and Henry, whose fine journal and gift for writing went unrecognized within her lifetime.

Typeset and Designed by Mike Burton

Printed by Thomson-Shore
on 50% postconsumer recycled paper
processed chlorine-free